Original title:

Nightfall's Gentle Lullaby

Copyright © 2024 Creative Arts Management OÜ

All rights reserved.

Author: Riley Hawthorne

ISBN HARDBACK: 978-9916-90-692-7

ISBN PAPERBACK: 978-9916-90-693-4

The Night's Woven Harmony

In the dusk, the shadows sway,
Stars emerge to light the way.
Moonlight dances on the ground,
Whispers soft, a soothing sound.

Breeze caresses, gentle sigh,
Crickets play a lullaby.
Night unfolds its velvet cloak,
In the stillness, dreams evoke.

Eager hearts in silence share,
Secrets linger in the air.
Time stands still, a moment caught,
In the peace that night has brought.

Fading day, with colors bold,
Night's embrace begins to hold.
In the dark, we find our peace,
As the world around us sleeps.

A Tapestry of Soft Twilight

Twilight weaves a gentle breeze,
Whispering through the swaying trees.
Colors mingle in the sky,
As day bids sweet goodbye.

Soft hues blend with fading light,
Birds retreat, it feels just right.
Stars begin their nightly gleam,
In this calm, we dare to dream.

Moonlit paths invite our tread,
By the light that softly spread.
Nature's hush, a tender call,
In this twilight, we stand tall.

Every heartbeat finds its tune,
Underneath the watchful moon.
In this tapestry, we roam,
Finding warmth, we feel at home.

Twilight's Embrace of Dreams

In twilight's glow, the shadows play,
As whispers weave through fading day.
The sky adorns a painted hue,
While stars awaken, fresh and new.

With gentle sighs, the world will melt,
In secrets soft, our hearts are felt.
A dance of night, a tender song,
In dreams we drift, where we belong.

The Soft Embrace of Night

The night unfolds its velvet cloak,
As silent stars begin to poke.
Their light like diamonds, faintly glow,
In this calm hour, time moves slow.

Whispers carried on the breeze,
The shadows sway among the trees.
In this embrace, we find our peace,
As all our worries find release.

Rest Beneath the Starry Dome

Beneath the dome of endless skies,
Where twinkling lights begin to rise.
Rest your head and close your eyes,
Let dreams take flight like butterflies.

The world will pause, its noise will cease,
In this stillness, find your peace.
With every breath, the night unfolds,
A tapestry of dreams retold.

A Gentle Closing of Eyes

A gentle hush envelops all,
As evening's charm begins to call.
With every blink, let worries fade,
In twilight's magic, be unmade.

The moonlight dances on the ground,
In soothing tones, a soft surround.
Embrace the night, let go of strife,
For in this moment, find your life.

Twilight's Caress on Weary Eyes

As daylight fades with gentle grace,
The world is wrapped in soft embrace.
Colors blend in whispered sighs,
A soothing balm for weary eyes.

Stars awaken, shy and bright,
Cascading down through velvet night.
The moon above, a silver prize,
Casting dreams where silence lies.

Echoes of the Sleepy Horizon

The sun dips low, a golden hue,
Where shadows stretch, the night feels new.
Whispers float on zephyr's breath,
In twilight's arms, we find our rest.

The horizon sings a lullaby,
Echoes of day as it bids goodbye.
Stars twinkle soft, like distant ties,
In the embrace of night, hope flies.

The Gentle Rhythm of Dusk

A heartbeat slows, the world does pause,
In evening's light, we find our flaws.
Crickets chirp, a serenade,
In the calm, our worries fade.

The sky blushes in twilight's art,
As day departs, we feel its heart.
Moments linger, time complies,
In dusky hush, our spirit tries.

Serenade of Moonbeams and Dreams

In the stillness, moonlight gleams,
A serenade of whispered dreams.
Soft shadows dance, the night is young,
As lullabies of stars are sung.

The world transformed in silver glow,
Where fantasies and wishes flow.
In dreams we soar, in darkness' guise,
Bathed in the light from loving skies.

Sleep's Soft Embrace

In twilight's glow, the world does cease,
The whispering hush brings gentle peace.
Cradled by dreams, we softly sway,
In sleep's warm arms, we drift away.

Each shadow dances, lightly twirled,
As night unfolds its secret world.
With every sigh, our troubles fade,
In sleep's soft arms, we are remade.

Stars Beneath a Velvet Sky

Glistening jewels in dark expanse,
The stars invite us to take a chance.
Each twinkle tells a tale of old,
Of dreams and wishes yet untold.

A tapestry of light so rare,
We gaze in awe, lost in our stare.
Beneath the heavens, hearts align,
In every spark, our hopes entwine.

Driftwood Reveries at Dusk

Upon the shore, where waves do lap,
Driftwood stories in twilight nap.
Each piece, a memory carved by time,
Whispers of dreams in rhythmic rhyme.

As dusk unfolds with gentle grace,
The horizon wears a dusky lace.
In each soft crash, old tales we find,
Nature's echo calls to the mind.

Lull of the Starlit Breeze

The night breeze hums a soothing tune,
Wrapped in a cloak of silver moon.
A tender whisper sweeps the trees,
In harmony, we find our ease.

The world is hushed, a lullaby,
As constellations dot the sky.
Each breath we take is filled with dreams,
In nature's arms, our spirit gleams.

Whispers from the Veil of Night

In the quiet, dreams take flight,
Softly woven, spun from light.
A whisper drifts on the breeze,
Carried gently through the trees.

Moonlight paints the world in gray,
Silent secrets start to play.
Stars above begin to gleam,
Cradling every tender dream.

Dusk's Embrace in Silken Silence

Dusk descends with gentle grace,
A soft hush fills the space.
Silken shadows blend and twine,
Nature sighs, the day's benign.

As the sun begins to fade,
Colors mix, a dusky shade.
Whispers linger in the air,
Wrapping night with gentle care.

Shadows Dance to the Call of Night

Shadows dance beneath the moon,
In the stillness, night's sweet tune.
They sway softly, twirl and spin,
Inviting dreams to drift within.

Mysterious tales begin to weave,
In the dark, all souls believe.
A haunting melody takes flight,
Echoing through the endless night.

Twilight's Tapestry of Rest

Twilight threads the sky with gold,
Wrapping night in secrets untold.
Fading light begins to blend,
As one chapter meets its end.

Rest your thoughts on gentle streams,
Let them float on evening dreams.
Cradle hopes in twilight's arms,
Safe from day's relentless charms.

Serenade of the Stars

Beneath the velvet night, they gleam,
Whispers of dreams in cosmic stream.
Each spark a tale, a wish to share,
In silence wrapped, with gentle care.

The moonlight dances on the sea,
Creating magic, wild and free.
While shadows play, the night does sing,
A serenade the heavens bring.

Silver Shadows Dance

In dusk's embrace, the silver glows,
Dancing shadows in mystic flows.
They weave through trees, a lover's waltz,
Enchanting night with secret faults.

Stars ignite the fabric of night,
Calls of spirits in their flight.
Whispers echo through the air,
In silver hues, we find our prayer.

Hushed Murmurs of Evening

As daylight fades, the murmurs rise,
Softly spoken, like tender sighs.
A hush envelops the moonlit ground,
In whispers lost, the night is found.

Crickets serenade the twilight,
While fireflies twinkle, pure delight.
The world slows down, we breathe it in,
In evening's grace, we find our kin.

Cradle of the Moon

A gentle cradle in night's embrace,
The moon shines down, a silver face.
It rocks the world in dreams so deep,
As stars above, their vigil keep.

In shadows cast, we find our way,
Through whispered thoughts at close of day.
Each heartbeat syncs with whispered tune,
In the soft light of the moon.

The Transitioning Sky

Daylight whispers dreams so fair,
Clouds dance gently in the air.
Colors blend, a painter's sigh,
In the midst, the sun waves bye.

Golden hues and shadows play,
As twilight claims the fleeting day.
Stars peek out, a shy debut,
In the sky, their glimmers blue.

Canvas of Night's Palette

A canvas draped in velvet dark,
Whispers secrets, leaves a mark.
Silver brushstrokes outline grace,
As the moon takes her rightful place.

Brush of starlight, soft and bright,
Paints the canvas of the night.
Each twinkle tells a tale untold,
In shadows deep, their dreams unfold.

Echoes of a Fading Sun

The sun sinks low, a fiery ball,
Casting shadows, a silent call.
Echoes linger in the breeze,
Whispering tales among the trees.

As warmth fades into cool night's grip,
Star-laden seas begin to dip.
In twilight's glow, the echoes stay,
Memories of a brighter day.

In the Embrace of Darkness

Embraced by night, the quiet hum,
A lullaby as shadows come.
Crickets sing in hushed delight,
In the arms of the soothing night.

Beneath the stars, the world slows down,
In darkness, no hint of a frown.
Embracing all that feels so right,
In the warm depths of gentle night.

Echoing Shadows of Serenity

In quiet woods where whispers weave,
The shadows dance, a gentle leave.
Beneath the boughs, the calm unfolds,
As nature's breath the heart enfolds.

A fleeting mist, a soft embrace,
In twilight's glow, we find our place.
Around us swirls the night's perfume,
A serenade within the gloom.

These echoing dreams, so bittersweet,
In silent prayers, our souls shall meet.
Each moment lost, but not in vain,
For in the shadows, peace remains.

Together here, we cast our fears,
In shadowed realms, through quiet tears.
With every breath, serenity,
In echoing shadows, we are free.

The Final Bow of Day

The sun dips low, the sky ablaze,
In golden hues, we lose the haze.
With twilight's kiss, the world transforms,
As dusk unfurls its velvet charms.

Soft whispers play on evening air,
A tender song, a lover's care.
With every glow, the stars ignite,
The final bow of fading light.

The horizon sighs, a gentle rest,
As night descends, we feel its jest.
In shadows long, our thoughts cascade,
The music of the night is made.

We hold the dusk, so soft, so near,
In this embrace, we shed our fear.
With every heartbeat, time slows down,
In twilight's arms, we wear the crown.

Glistening Hush of Twilight

As day concedes to night's embrace,
The stars appear, a jeweled lace.
In tranquil hush, the world's at peace,
In twilight's grip, our cares release.

The sky ignites with colors rare,
A canvas painted, beyond compare.
Each glowing hue a sweet goodbye,
As day gives way to night's soft sigh.

The breeze carries a whispered tune,
A serenade beneath the moon.
With every breath, the shadows play,
In glistening hush, we drift away.

Here in this space, we find our way,
Through twilight's arms, we long to stay.
In moments caught between day and night,
The glistening hush brings pure delight.

Lull of the Crescent Moon

The crescent moon hangs soft and low,
Its gentle light, a silver glow.
In dreamy realms, our spirits soar,
As night unfolds, we yearn for more.

The stars align in silent prayer,
While nightingale sings sweet despair.
In whispers soft, the world finds rest,
In lullabies, our hearts are blessed.

The shadows weave a soothing rhyme,
In lull of night, we trap the time.
With every sigh, the darkness pleads,
In crescent light, our silence leads.

Embraced by night, we drift away,
In serenades where dreams will play.
With every breath, a story spun,
In lull of the moon, we become one.

A Dance Beneath the Moonlight

In shadows deep, where whispers play,
The night unveils its soft ballet.
With silver beams that softly gleam,
We sway together, lost in dream.

The stars above, like diamonds bright,
Guide our feet in gentle flight.
Each twirl and spin, a sweet embrace,
In this enchanted, timeless space.

The cool breeze hums a lullaby,
As we lose track of time, nearby.
In moonlit glow, our hearts align,
A dance of souls, forever twine.

Cradled in Evening's Glow

The sun dips low, the skies ignite,
Painting hues of gold and light.
Soft whispers drift on summer air,
Cradling dreams without a care.

With each moment, time stands still,
As twilight wraps the world in chill.
The stars awake, a twinkling sigh,
While shadows dance, and wish to fly.

Through fragile wings of evening's grace,
We find our solace, our embrace.
Beneath the heavens, hearts in flow,
Forever lost, cradled in glow.

The Soothing Veil

A gentle mist, the morning sighs,
Cascading soft from cloudy skies.
It wraps around in tender care,
A soothing veil over the air.

With every breath, a calm descends,
As whispers ride the breeze, my friend.
The world awakens, slow and kind,
In the embrace of peace we find.

Each droplet sparkles, fresh with grace,
Reflecting light in every place.
Nature hums a tranquil tune,
As hearts unite beneath the moon.

A Gentle Descent into Quiet

As dusk descends, the world grows still,
A tranquil peace begins to fill.
With heavy eyes and whispered dreams,
The night reveals its subtle gleams.

In shadows deep, we find our rest,
Where silence wraps, and feels the best.
The stars awake, a watchful guard,
While time drifts on, both sweet and hard.

Each moment fades, a soft goodbye,
As night unfolds its velvet sky.
In this embrace, we lose the fight,
And gently sink into the night.

The Subtle Shift to Night

The sun dips low, the day retreats,
Shadows stretch across the streets.
Whispers of dusk begin to play,
As brightened skies turn shades of gray.

Chirping crickets start their song,
Nature's orchestra plays along.
The air grows cool, a gentle breeze,
Sways the branches of the trees.

Softly falls the velvet cloak,
Embracing all, as stillness spoke.
The world slows down, a quiet breath,
In peaceful moments, life finds rest.

Stars awaken, one by one,
In the vast expanse, their dance begun.
Nighttime's charm, a soothing sight,
In the subtle shift to night.

Gentle Tones of Twilight

Soft hues blend in the evening sky,
Golden warmth as day waves goodbye.
Mountains silhouette, dark against light,
As whispers of the dusk take flight.

Crimson petals close their bloom,
Familiar scents dispel the gloom.
A lullaby of colors blend,
Where day and night, in peace, suspend.

The cool air carries promise near,
Of dreams unveiled, and hopes sincere.
Deep breaths of calm, the heart knows best,
In gentle tones, we find our rest.

Stars begin to twinkle bright,
Guiding souls through the night.
With every shade that dims the fight,
We embrace the gentle twilight.

The Nighttime's Promise

The moon ascends, a silver grace,
Illuminating every space.
Promises whispered on the air,
Of dreams fulfilled beyond despair.

Each glimmer speaks of tales untold,
Of love ignited, of hearts so bold.
In shadows deep, new paths arise,
Underneath the starlit skies.

With every hour that drifts away,
Freed from the burdens of the day.
The nighttime holds a sacred trust,
In every heartbeat, hope is bust.

Cradled in calm, we dare to dream,
Embracing light in every beam.
Through darkest skies, we'll find our way,
In the nighttime's promise, we'll stay.

Serenitee among Stars

In the quiet glow of the night,
Stars gather round, a dazzling sight.
Whispers of peace in the silence reign,
As we wander, free from pain.

A soft breeze dances through the trees,
Carrying with it the softest pleas.
Dreams linger in the starlit haze,
As we drift in time's gentle ways.

Each twinkle holds a story dear,
Of wishes made, of love sincere.
In this realm where hearts align,
Serenity found, perfectly divine.

With every spark, a fire ignites,
Leading us through wondrous nights.
In this harmony beneath the skies,
We find our place where magic lies.

Whispers of the Twilight Serenade

In the garden where shadows play,
The twilight whispers secrets low,
Gentle breezes softly sway,
As stars begin their evening show.

Crickets sing their evening song,
While fireflies dance in delight,
The world turns quiet, calm, and strong,
As day gives way to gentle night.

The moon rises, a silver crown,
Casting light on the soft grass,
In this moment, I won't drown,
I'll stay here, let the stillness pass.

With every breath, the night unfolds,
A melody of peace and grace,
In twilight's arms, the heart beholds,
A serenade, a warm embrace.

Cradle of the Dusk's Embrace

In the cradle where day meets night,
The sun dips low, kisses the trees,
Colors blend in fading light,
A gentle hush upon the breeze.

The sky ignites with hues so warm,
As clouds drift softly overhead,
Nature wraps in twilight's charm,
While dreams awaken, lightly spread.

Stars peek out from their velvet shrouds,
The moon unveils its silken glow,
In this sanctuary of clouds,
The heart finds peace, as rivers flow.

With every sigh, the evening calls,
Inviting souls to linger here,
In dusk's embrace, as daylight falls,
A sacred moment, crystal clear.

Moonlit Dreams on Silver Waves

Upon the shore where whispers dwell,
The silver waves caress the land,
Underneath the moon's soft spell,
I sink into dreams, hand in hand.

The ocean sings its lullaby,
As stars twinkle in the night air,
A tranquil dance where time slips by,
Cradled in the love we share.

The horizon glows with hopes anew,
Each crest of wave a secret told,
In moonlit dreams, our spirits flew,
A treasure more than silver and gold.

Around us swirls a magic mist,
Where memories fade and laughter plays,
In this moment, I can't resist,
A journey set on silver waves.

The Hush of Evening Shadows

In the hush where shadows blend,
The day whispers its last goodbye,
As twilight folds, we can pretend,
To catch the dreams that softly fly.

The trees are silhouettes in gray,
Embracing stillness, calm and deep,
While night falls gently into play,
As memories stroll in their sleep.

Each breath brings forth a gentle peace,
As stars ignite the velvet dome,
In this quiet, worries cease,
And every heart can find its home.

In the shadows, secrets bloom,
Wrapped in night's enchanting fold,
The hush prevails, dispelling gloom,
In whispers soft, our tales unfold.

Slumbering Skies

Clouds drift softly, whispers sigh,
Stars peek gently, twinkling high.
Moonlit paths in shadows gleam,
Nighttime wraps us in a dream.

Waves of calm in twilight's glow,
Secrets hidden, soft winds flow.
Silhouettes of trees stand tall,
Nature's cradle, a soothing call.

From afar, the nightbird sings,
Beneath the sky, the magic clings.
As darkness falls, we close our eyes,
In slumber's arms, the world complies.

Sleep beckons with its gentle grace,
In every heart, a resting place.
Skies above, so vast and deep,
Cradle us in peaceful sleep.

The Calm Before Sleep

Crickets chirp in soft refrain,
Daylight fades, it's time to wane.
Shadows stretch across the ground,
In this hush, peace can be found.

Gentle breezes brush the leaves,
In stillness, the heart believes.
The world slows, the chaos fades,
As calm wraps us in its shades.

Flickering candles, warm and bright,
Creating dreams that dance in light.
Tomorrow waits, but now's the hour,
To bask within a tranquil power.

As night descends and stars align,
In silence, we draw soft divine.
The calm before, a tender sweep,
Inviting all to gently sleep.

Dreams in the Twilight

Twilight whispers, shadows play,
Colors blend, end of the day.
Dreams awaken in the soft light,
Filling hearts through the night.

Crescent moon with silver rays,
Guides us through this gentle haze.
In the quiet, magic brews,
Embracing hope in twilight's cues.

Memories dance in evening's grace,
Each thought a bright, enchanting trace.
We float on clouds of tender dreams,
Wrapped in warmth that softly gleams.

With every heartbeat, love will grow,
Through twilight's charm, we softly flow.
In this moment, pure and right,
We find our dreams in the twilight.

Evening's Softest Sigh

As daylight wanes, the night arrives,
An orchestra of lullabies.
Whispers float in dusk's embrace,
Painting peace on every face.

The horizon blushes, soft and wide,
Hiding secrets the stars provide.
Nature holds her breath in awe,
In evening's beauty, hearts withdraw.

The world is cloaked in soothing song,
Where every shadow can belong.
With open arms, the night will greet,
Each moment gentle, pure and sweet.

So close your eyes, let worries fly,
Within the stillness, raise a sigh.
Evening's breath, a tender balm,
Lulls us with its softest calm.

The Lull of Dusk's Quietude

When shadows stretch and whispers blend,
The world slows down as day must end.
A soft embrace of twilight's hue,
In silence nature bids adieu.

The breeze, it sighs a soothing song,
While crickets join, where night belongs.
The stars appear with gentle grace,
In this serene, enchanted space.

A calm descends, the heart will rest,
Each beating pulse, a quiet quest.
In dusk's embrace, all fears released,\nIn stillness, find your inner peace.

Fading Light's Gentle Kiss

The sun dips low, a glowing sphere,
Its warmth retreats, but draws us near.
With colors bold, the canvas paints,
As day concedes, the night awaits.

Soft hues of orange turn to gray,
The vibrant world begins to sway.
Each fleeting moment whispers low,
In fading light, let worries go.

With gentle touch, the stars ignite,
They twinkle softly through the night.
In every blink, a dream descends,
As darkness wraps, the day now ends.

The Calm Before the Starry Dream

In twilight's hush, the world lies still,
Anticipation, a quiet thrill.
The stars prepare to light the sky,
In whispered hopes, we breathe a sigh.

Each shadow casts a gentle spell,
As time slows down, all is well.
The moon awakes, pale and bright,
A guiding glow through velvet night.

The calm before the dreams unfold,
With secrets waiting to be told.
In silent moments, hearts will soar,
To realms unseen, we long to explore.

Evening's Warble of Tranquility

As daylight fades, the evening sings,
A chorus soft of tranquil things.
The world is wrapped in gentle peace,
With nature's hymn, our cares release.

The leaves dance lightly in the breeze,
While nightingale croons through the trees.
The heart finds solace in the sound,
Where joy and stillness can be found.

With every note, the soul takes flight,
Through calmness shared in the dim light.
As evening warbles sweet and clear,
We cradle dreams, and hold them dear.

Driftwood of Dreams

Waves whisper tales of old,
Driftwood drifts with secrets untold.
A journey carved in the sea,
Where dreams float wild and free.

In the twilight's soft embrace,
Memories find their place.
Echoes of laughter and sighs,
Beneath the painted skies.

Tides shall pull, tides shall let go,
Each tale unwinds like a bow.
Carried forth on currents strong,
In sleep's sweet cradle, belong.

As dawn breaks, shadows depart,
Dreams weave close to the heart.
Driftwood settles, quiet and still,
As life's adventure bends to will.

Evening's Tender Touch

The sun dips low, casting gold,
Evening whispers, soft and bold.
Stars awaken in the night,
Dreams begin their gentle flight.

With every sigh, the world slows,
In moonlight's glow, warmth bestows.
Crickets serenade the hush,
In twilight's peaceful, sweet rush.

A breeze carries the scent of pine,
Nature's beauty, so divine.
Close your eyes, feel the embrace,
As night descends with gentle grace.

Hold this moment, let it stay,
In evening's arms, drift away.
With tender touch, the night does weave,
A peaceful heart, we shall believe.

Lullaby of the Starlit Veil

Underneath the starlit sky,
Whispers float, a soothing sigh.
Dreamers gather, hearts entwined,
In the night, true peace we find.

Stars like diamonds softly gleam,
Guiding us through every dream.
Wrapped in night's gentle embrace,
We wander forth to seek our place.

Each twinkle tells a story bright,
In the cradle of the night.
Breathe in deep and let love flow,
In this lullaby, we grow.

As the world slips into peace,
All our worries find release.
In the starlit veil, we lay,
Dreaming of a new today.

Soothing Stars Above

Soothing stars in skies aglow,
Whisper secrets from below.
Each twinkle sings a melody,
A soft hymn to you and me.

In the canvas of the night,
Constellations dance in light.
Hearts entwined under the dome,
Lost together, far from home.

Breath by breath, we share this view,
In the quiet, love feels new.
Let the cosmos guide our way,
In this moment, we shall stay.

As dreams unfold like petals bright,
Soothing stars adorn the night.
With every blink, a wish is cast,
In this stillness, peace will last.

A Peaceful Unraveling in the Dark

In shadows deep where silence grows,
The stars awake, their soft light flows.
A tranquil breath, the world stands still,
In night's embrace, the heart can heal.

The moon unfolds its silver thread,
Where dreams and hopes are gently spread.
In whispered thoughts, we find our way,
A peaceful arc at end of day.

With every sigh, the darkness glows,
A dance of time that gently flows.
In hidden realms, the secrets hum,
As night unfolds, the peace will come.

So close your eyes, let worries part,
Embrace the calm that fills your heart.
In this unraveling, softly hark,
Find solace deep, a light in dark.

The Pause of Night's Sweet Song.

The night falls heavy, still and sweet,
With whispered lullabies that greet.
Each star a note in velvet sky,
In harmony, they drift and fly.

The world below, a hushed refrain,
While moonlight weaves a soft caress.
In moments paused, all fears remain,
Wrapped in the night's soft, warm finesse.

A gentle breeze stirs with intent,
It carries dreams from far away.
Each sigh of night, a sweet lament,
In silent dark, we wish and stay.

So listen close, let echoes rise,
To find the peace in nightly sighs.
For in this pause, deep breaths prolong,
We find our place, in night's sweet song.

Whispers of the Dusk

As dusk descends, the colors blend,
A painter's brush with no end.
Soft whispers weave through trees so tall,
In twilight's grasp, we heed the call.

The sun retreats with golden rays,
While shadows stretch in playful ways.
A gentle hush, the world at rest,
In evening's arms, we feel so blessed.

The stars prepare for their debut,
As twilight whispers all that's true.
A secret dance of dusk's delight,
Where day meets night in soft twilight.

So linger long, embrace the dusk,
And find the magic in the husk.
In whispered tones, let peace emerge,
As night unfolds, the senses surge.

Twilight's Embrace

In twilight's glow, the world transforms,
A blend of colors, night performs.
The sky adorned with hues so bright,
Inviting dreams to take their flight.

With gentle touch, the shadows creep,
As day drifts close to slumber's keep.
A symphony of soft goodbye,
While whispers hum and breezes sigh.

The horizon glows with amber light,
In tranquil moments, hearts take flight.
Through dusk's embrace, we find our way,
A promise held in the fading day.

So hold this hour, let silence bloom,
In twilight's arms, dispel the gloom.
For in this space, our dreams arise,
And dance beneath the evening skies.

A Gentle Rhyme for Wandering Souls

Beneath the stars, we drift afar,
In twilight's glow, we find our star.
Each whispered breeze, a tale unfolds,
Of dreams and paths that courage holds.

Through fields of gold, our laughter flows,
In search of light where kindness grows.
With every step, the heart aligns,
A gentle rhyme, in life's designs.

In shadows deep, where echoes play,
We seek the dawn of a new day.
Embrace the warmth, the love we share,
For wandering souls, the journey's fair.

So hand in hand, we chase the light,
Through vibrant colors of the night.
A melody, both soft and sweet,
In gentle rhymes, our souls do meet.

The Lattice of Night's Soft Whisper

In shadows spun, the night does weave,
A lattice where our hearts believe.
The softest whispers call us near,
And wrap our dreams in silent cheer.

Stars twinkle bright in velvet skies,
Their shimmering light, a soft reprise.
The moonlit path invites us close,
To dance with night, our secret dose.

With every sigh, the twilight sings,
Unraveling time on feathered wings.
The gentle hush of night bestows,
A balm for weary hearts that chose.

And as we rest beneath the glow,
The lattice weaves a tale we know.
In whispered tones, our spirits soar,
For in the night, we seek for more.

Slumbering under Celestial Canopies

Under the stars, we dream and sigh,
Embraced by night, we let time fly.
Celestial canopies spread wide,
A safe retreat where hopes reside.

With each soft breath, the cosmos hums,
A lullaby where starlight comes.
We close our eyes, the world fades gray,
In slumber's arms, we drift away.

Bathed in light of distant flames,
The universe calls us by name.
Each twinkling star, a wish we weave,
Sanctuary where hearts believe.

In silent dreams, we find our way,
Through timeless realms where shadows play.
Slumbering here, our souls unite,
Under the watch of endless night.

Evenfall's Solace in Stillness

As daylight wanes, we pause to breathe,
In evenfall's embrace, we cleave.
The softest hush descends like dew,
In stillness found, we start anew.

The golden hues of sun retreat,
While twilight wraps the world in heat.
Each breath we take, a moment's grace,
In evening's glow, we find our place.

With gentle whispers, night shall fall,
In silent hearts, we hear the call.
The solace found in fading light,
Guides us through the velvet night.

In the stillness, we shall find,
The peace that lingers, intertwined.
Evenfall's gift, a soft embrace,
A serenade of time and space.

The Darkening Sky's Secrets

Whispers ride the dusky air,
Stars flicker, secrets loom bare.
Shadows dance with silent grace,
Night reveals a hidden face.

Clouds gather, a tapestry spun,
Veiling the light of the waning sun.
In twilight's breath, mysteries call,
Darkening skies, a shrouded thrall.

Beneath the moon's soft embrace,
Dreams awaken in darkened space.
Ancient tales and echoes blend,
In the night where shadows bend.

Hearts beat in the silence deep,
In the dark, the world will sleep.
Yet within the night's caress,
Lie the stars' soft, secret mess.

Crescendo of the Midnight Hour

The clock strikes twelve with a gentle sigh,
Echoes of dreams that drift and fly.
In the stillness, we hear the song,
A melody that feels so strong.

Notes unfurl in the velvet night,
A tapestry woven with pure delight.
With every breath, the moments bloom,
The midnight hour dispels all gloom.

Voices blend in a whispered tune,
Moonlit dancers sway to the rune.
Hearts entwined, in rhythms clear,
As the midnight's magic draws us near.

Time slows down in this sacred space,
Where shadows and light find their place.
A crescendo flows in the soft night air,
In the depths of silence, dreams laid bare.

Sweet Murmurs of the Unseen

Gentle whispers ride the breeze,
Carrying tales through the swaying trees.
In the quiet, secrets unfurl,
From the heart of the unseen world.

Echoing soft in the twilight dim,
A lullaby sung on a breezy whim.
Though elusive, their grace we feel,
Sweet murmurs linger, tender and real.

The night cradles each hidden sigh,
Under the vast and watchful sky.
In shadows cast, we softly tread,
Chasing the whispers that dance ahead.

Every heartbeat, a story told,
In invisible ink, life's joys unfold.
Listen closely, let your heart glean,
The sweet murmurs of the unseen.

Restful Rhythms Beneath the Stars

In the quiet of night, soft and kind,
Restful rhythms to the heart aligned.
Stars flicker in patterns like dreams,
As the world hushes and gently gleams.

Crickets chirp in a lullaby tone,
Guiding the weary, the lost, the alone.
With every breath, we drift and sway,
In the cradle of night, we find our way.

The cosmos hums its soothing song,
In the vastness where we belong.
Under the night sky's watchful glance,
In restful rhythms, we find our dance.

Wrapped in the night's serene guise,
We journey through this starlit surprise.
In every heartbeat, a promise lies,
Restful rhythms beneath the skies.

Celestial Tapestry

Stars weave dreams in the night sky,
Threads of light in a darkened sea.
Whispers of cosmos softly sigh,
Painting tales of what's yet to be.

Galaxies dance with a gentle grace,
Spirals of fate entwined and spun.
Each little spark finds its own place,
A tapestry bright—a world begun.

Nebulas bloom in colors so rare,
Clouds of stardust drift through the void.
In this vastness, we find love and care,
In cosmic arms, our dreams enjoyed.

Time unfolds like a scroll unrolled,
Every moment a page anew.
In the tapestry bright, stories told,
Celestial wonders bring life to you.

Veil of the Nocturne

Moonlight spills on the quiet earth,
A silver shroud of whispered dreams.
Echoed tales of love and mirth,
Flow softly through the midnight streams.

Night wraps all in its gentle fold,
Stars blink softly, a glance, a wink.
In shadows deep, secrets unfold,
Thoughts linger long for time to think.

Breezes carry the scent of night,
Glimmers of hope in the dark play.
Nature whispers in soft delight,
As the world sleeps, dreams drift away.

The veil of night, a calming friend,
Inviting hearts to pause and rest.
In the quiet, the whispers blend,
Embraced by darkness, feel the blessed.

Shadows Wrap the World

Darkness spills where light once shone,
Shadows creep at the fall of day.
In the quiet, the heart feels lone,
As the bright fades, the colors gray.

Whispers linger in the twilight air,
Figures dance on the edge of sight.
A shiver flows through the evening fair,
As the world wraps in folds of night.

Gentle lingering of faded dreams,
Beneath the branches, echoes call.
In tall shadows, a soft moonbeam,
Guides the lost through the night's thrall.

Yet in the dark, there's a spark so bright,
A flicker of hope in the black sea.
Shadows wrap but do not incite,
Inner strength blooms wild and free.

Woven in Midnight's Embrace

Midnight weaves its silent spell,
Threads of dreams in the stillness spin.
In the quiet, all secrets dwell,
Whispers of night invite us in.

Stars hang low like lanterns bright,
Guiding the heart through the shadowed trails.
In each pause, we find pure light,
Stitched with hope in the nightingales.

Breath of night wraps the weary soul,
Cradling thoughts in a soft embrace.
In the dark, we find ourselves whole,
In midnight's arms, we find our place.

The world slows down beneath the moon,
Time suspends its hurried race.
In the quiet, a soft tune,
Woven lovingly in night's grace.

A Soothing Solstice

In the calm of night's embrace,
Stars twinkle with gentle grace.
Whispers of the cool night air,
Nature's peace, beyond compare.

Moonlight bathes the tranquil land,
Guiding dreams with its soft hand.
Solstice warmth and shadows blend,
A perfect night, as day must end.

Lulled by crickets, hearts unite,
Together under starlit light.
Memories of the sun's bright reign,
Wrapped in darkness, free from pain.

Softly fading, echoes sing,
Of the joy that night can bring.
Embrace the quiet, breathe it in,
For in this peace, our souls begin.

Mellow Hues of Dusk

Golden rays begin to fade,
Drawing close the evening shade.
Crimson clouds dance in the sky,
As daylight waves its soft goodbye.

Whispers of the closing day,
In twilight's warmth, we find our way.
Reflections on the water's face,
Hold the beauty of this place.

Gentle breezes start to stir,
While fading tunes begin to purr.
Nature's palette, rich and deep,
In dusky tones, our hearts will leap.

As stars above begin to gleam,
We weave together our shared dream.
In the stillness, time will pause,
Embracing dusk without a cause.

Dawn's Cousin in Retreat

The day slips softly into night,
With shadows drawing out of sight.
In the twilight, time takes flight,
While whispers fade, and spirits heighten.

Cool embrace of evening's breath,
Stirs the heart, a dance with death.
The colors fade, a gentle call,
A moment's hush before the fall.

Lingering light begins to wane,
Sinking deep into the grain.
Stars awaken, bright and bold,
In this retreat, a story told.

In the quiet, dreams will bloom,
While silver beams dispel the gloom.
As darkness wraps the world in peace,
The heart's wild longing will not cease.

Chasing the Last Light

Footsteps quicken on the shore,
As daylight bids its proud encore.
Golden beams like fleeting dreams,
Elude the grasp, or so it seems.

Cool winds carry hints of night,
While shadows dance, avoiding light.
The sky ignites in fiery hues,
As we pursue the day's soft dues.

In the chase, our spirits soar,
Yearning for that which came before.
With every moment slipping by,
We reach to touch the evening sky.

Yet as we run, we learn to find,
The beauty in what's left behind.
For even in the dark, we glow,
Chasing the light, forever slow.

Lull before the Dark

Whispers of the night entwine,
Softly brushing against the pine.
Stars awaken, quiet sighs,
As daylight's warmth begins to die.

A hush falls over distant hills,
Embracing calm, the silence fills.
Birds retreat, the moonlight gleams,
In the cradle of fading dreams.

Shadows stretch, as twilight fades,
In the coolness, comfort wades.
Hope lingers in the evening air,
A tranquil peace beyond compare.

Let the heart beat slow and low,
In the lull, let worries go.
For soon the stars will gently spark,
And all will rest before the dark.

Gentle Tides of Night

The moon drapes silver on the sea,
Waves murmur soft, a lullaby free.
Stars twinkle like distant guides,
In the gentle tides where magic hides.

Crickets serenade under the sky,
As shadows dance and dreams fly high.
The night breathes slow, a tender embrace,
In every pulse, a hidden grace.

Clouds drift softly, cotton-like,
Casting dreams on the midnight hike.
Whispers echo amongst the trees,
Carried gently by the evening breeze.

As the world sleeps in twilight's arms,
Surrendering to the night's soft charms,
Find solace in the quiet flow,
Of gentle tides that come and go.

The Embrace of Shadows

Shadows gather 'neath the moon,
Wrapping the earth in a soft tune.
Whispers weave through the chill air,
As night unfolds its tender care.

The world retreats from amber glow,
Embraced by darkness, soft and slow.
Stars peer down with watchful eyes,
Guarding secrets where silence lies.

Every rustle, every sigh,
A promise made beneath the sky.
In the quiet, a heart finds peace,
As worries of the day release.

In shadows deep, where dreams ignite,
We find our way through velvet night.
Let whispers guide us on this quest,
In the embrace, we find our rest.

Night's Celestial Serenade

In the night, a symphony starts,
Stars strum soft on heaven's harps.
Melodies drift on cool, dark air,
Music cradled in moon's fair glare.

Gentle whispers, a twilight song,
Echo around where we belong.
Each note dances, a silver glide,
Through the universe, far and wide.

Dreams unfold like petals bright,
In the stillness of the night.
With every breath, the soul takes flight,
On the wings of peace, pure delight.

Listen close to the stars' refrain,
Let your heart feel the soft rain.
For in this serenade of night,
We find our truths, our spirits' light.

An Evening's Invitation

As the sun begins to fade,
Whispers of twilight invade,
Stars start to twinkle and gleam,
In this magical evening dream.

Softly the breeze begins to play,
Inviting the night to sway,
Come take a stroll, feel the cheer,
An evening full of wonder is near.

Crickets chirp in lilting tune,
Under the watchful gaze of the moon,
Every shadow dances along,
While we hum our softest song.

Join this quiet, serene sight,
As the day turns slow to night,
Together we'll weave our delight,
An evening's invitation feels just right.

Haze of the Night's Breath

Silent whispers in the air,
Mystery draped everywhere,
A haze hangs low, soft and light,
As shadows blend with the night.

Stars twinkle in the vast sky,
While moonbeams gently sigh,
Every moment wrapped in bliss,
In the stillness, dreams we kiss.

Fog caresses the sleeping land,
Holding secrets in its hand,
Nature speaks in hushed tones,
In the world where night has grown.

Let your worries drift away,
In the night's sweet ballet,
In the haze that softly flows,
Embrace the magic that night bestows.

Soothing the World to Sleep

Gentle lullabies start to play,
Calling the fleeting day,
Stars gather in the twilight,
To soothe the world into night.

Clouds, like pillows, drift above,
Wrapping all in tender love,
Shadows stretch and softly yawn,
Welcoming the dreamy dawn.

Crickets serenade the trees,
With whispers carried on the breeze,
As moonbeams light the silent glade,
In this peaceful masquerade.

Rest your heart, close your eyes,
Underneath the starlit skies,
In this calm, let worries sweep,
As we cradle the world to sleep.

Enchanted Shadows

Beneath the ancient, whispering trees,
Shadows dance with the softest ease,
Each flicker tells a tale untold,
In their embrace, mysteries unfold.

Glimmers of light, a fleeting glance,
Weaving through the twilight dance,
The night holds secrets, sweet and deep,
In enchanted shadows where dreams creep.

Footsteps soft on the forest floor,
Echoes of magic we can't ignore,
With every breath, a story flows,
Through enchanted whispers, the night glows.

Come wander where the shadows play,
Let them guide you on your way,
In the depths of night, we'll embrace,
The enchanting shadows we'll chase.

Melodies of the Dimming Light

Soft whispers fade in golden hue,
As shadows stretch, the day bids adieu.
A lullaby of stars starts to hum,
In the quiet, night's embrace will come.

Low notes linger in the twilight air,
Each fading ray, a gentle prayer.
Crickets sing as the world slows down,
In this moment, no hint of a frown.

The colors blend, a canvas divine,
Where nature's peace and stillness align.
Echoes of laughter from times now past,
In the warmth of dusk, memories cast.

Melodies float on the breath of night,
As dreams awaken beneath soft starlight.
Close your eyes, let the music play,
In the heart of dusk, forever stay.

The Quietude of Dusk

The sun dips low, a brush of fire,
In the hush, a softening choir.
Whispers of twilight, calm and deep,
In the stillness, the world takes a leap.

Branches sway in a tender sigh,
Underneath the vastening sky.
The colors fade, like fleeting tales,
As the evening's breath gently exhales.

A golden orb, the last light wanes,
Nature hums, and silence reigns.
Beneath the stars, we find our peace,
In the quietude, the heart's release.

Time stands still, wrapped in a shroud,
A tranquil space, away from the crowd.
With each heartbeat, the night draws near,
In the quietude, we lose our fear.

Carried by the Night's Breath

The night unfolds like a velvet sheet,
Cool breezes kiss, and shadows greet.
Stars emerge, like glimmers of hope,
In the dark, our spirits elope.

A symphony of crickets begins,
As the moon smiles, the magic spins.
Whispers of dreams float on soft winds,
With every heartbeat, a new story begins.

Through the stillness, time seems to bend,
Moments linger, as we transcend.
Carried by wonders that dance in the sky,
In the night's breath, we learn to fly.

Wrapped in the arms of the universe vast,
In a tapestry woven from dreams of the past.
The night speaks softly, with love and light,
Carried away by the breath of the night.

Echoes of the Falling Day

As daylight fades, shadows converge,
Colors dissolve in a gentle purge.
The air grows still in a lingering sigh,
Echoing softly as the sun says goodbye.

Footsteps quiet on paths of stone,
In the dusk, we wander alone.
Each echo carries tales of the light,
Whispers of love, glowing bright.

Fleeting moments like fireflies glow,
Filling our hearts with warmth from below.
The day surrenders to the night's claim,
In the echoes, we whisper your name.

With each heartbeat, the silence will grow,
As the stars weave stories we long to know.
In the embrace of the night's gentle sway,
We find solace in echoes of the falling day.

Starlit Reverie

In the quiet of the night,
Stars twinkle with delight.
Whispers dance upon the breeze,
Dreams flicker like the leaves.

Moonlight bathes the sleeping ground,
Magic threads all around.
Softly glows the azure sky,
As wishes glimmer and fly.

Time drifts gently, slow as rain,
With echoes of a sweet refrain.
Hearts take wing, they start to soar,
In starlit realms, forevermore.

Each twinkle speaks of hopes untold,
In silver threads, the night enfolds.
Let your spirit softly glide,
In this starlit reverie, abide.

Gentle Evening Ephemeris

The sun dips low, paints the sky,
With hues of gold that gently sigh.
Birds serenade as they retreat,
With melodies that echo sweet.

Crickets sing their twilight song,
As shadows stretch and night grows long.
The air, a tapestry of calm,
Wraps the world in evening's balm.

Each moment, fleeting, soft, and light,
In quiet whispers, dusk takes flight.
Nature pauses, breathes anew,
In sighs of peace, the stars breakthrough.

Time unwinds in this soft grace,
As darkness falls, night finds its place.
Behold this gentle, brief embrace,
In evening's dance, a tender space.

The Lull of the Sunset

In hues of crimson, gold, and rose,
The day whispers, and softly doze.
As shadows stretch, the light cascades,
Evening blood-orange gently fades.

Clouds embrace the sun's last glow,
Wrapping all in a warm tableau.
Day's soft sighs in twilight blend,
With promises of night descend.

The horizon, a painter's dream,
Where light and dark weave and beam.
A lullaby for hearts to rest,
In the sunset's arms, we are blessed.

With every flicker, time stands still,
As dusk, in grace, starts to fulfill.
In the night, new dreams take flight,
In the lull of the sunset light.

Murmurs of the Midnight Breeze

A whisper floats through moonlit air,
Carrying secrets everywhere.
It weaves through trees, so soft, so sly,
Awakens stars within the sky.

The world, at peace, in shadows deep,
Hushes low, as the night does seep.
Echoes blend with sighs of night,
In the dark, a soft delight.

The cool embrace of night's caress,
So tenderly, our hearts confess.
With every breath, the stillness grows,
In the murmurs, the mystery flows.

In midnight's cloak, we find our soul,
Wrapped in dreams, together whole.
Let the breeze weave stories sweet,
In the calmness, our hearts meet.

Shimmering Silhouettes

In twilight's glow, shadows play,
Whispers of night, chasing the day.
Figures dance in soft embrace,
Silhouettes shimmer, lost in grace.

Glimmers of hope on the horizon,
Dreams unfurl like wings of a swan.
Stories unfold in the evening air,
A world transformed, beyond compare.

Fleeting moments, a gentle sigh,
The stars awaken, lighting the sky.
Each flicker of light tells a tale,
Of shimmering souls that never pale.

As night descends with tender care,
Silhouettes linger, a breath of air.
In the quiet, we find our way,
To the heart of night, where dreams sway.

The Peace of Fading Light

Beneath the horizon, the sun dips low,
A gentle embrace, soft and slow.
Colors blend in a tranquil sky,
As day whispers its sweet goodbye.

The world exudes a soothing balm,
Harmony reigns, a moment of calm.
Birds find rest in the fading rays,
As twilight weaves its silken ways.

In the hush, the heart finds home,
Each glimmer of light, a reason to roam.
The peace of dusk, a cherished friend,
In its gentle arms, our worries mend.

So let us linger, time stands still,
In the fading light, we find our will.
Embracing the night, we softly sigh,
For in this peace, we learn to fly.

Restful Hours in Stillness

In the quiet wood, where shadows blend,
Time seems to pause, troubles suspend.
Crickets sing lullabies to the trees,
As the evening breathes with gentle ease.

Moonlight spills on the forest floor,
A silver quilt, nature's decor.
Restful hours in soft embrace,
In stillness, we find our hidden space.

Dreams take flight on the evening breeze,
Whispered secrets shared with the leaves.
Every sigh in the tranquil air,
Bears the promise of dreams laid bare.

In the hushed calm, let worries cease,
Bathed in serenity, we find peace.
In restful hours, the heart can mend,
Embracing stillness, our dearest friend.

The Calm of the Vanishing Sun

As daylight bids the world adieu,
The sky paints hues of deepening blue.
With every glance, the colors swirl,
In harmony, day starts to unfurl.

The sun sinks low, a fiery ball,
Casting warmth in its gentle fall.
In the calm, we find our place,
Wrapped in the soft, golden embrace.

Whispers of twilight brush the land,
As shadows merge with night so grand.
Each fleeting moment holds a spark,
Of memories carved in the coming dark.

In the stillness, fears take flight,
The calm of night brings sweet delight.
We watch as the sun bids its last shine,
And in this peace, our souls entwine.

The Dreamweaver's Caress

In the twilight's soft embrace,
Dreams unfold their tender grace.
Threads of silver gently weave,
Carving paths that we believe.

Stars align in whispered song,
Guiding souls where they belong.
Through the veil of night we float,
In the silence, hearts can gloat.

Winds of fate, they swirl and twine,
In the realms where shadows shine.
Sailing through the cosmos vast,
Every moment tethered fast.

So let the dreamweaver's light,
Lead us through the endless night.
In the depths of slumber's sea,
Find the truth that sets us free.

Whispers from the Dimming Horizon

As the day begins to wane,
Echoes speak of joy and pain.
Colors fade, the sun sinks low,
Nature's breath begins to slow.

Whispers carry on the breeze,
Swaying softly through the trees.
Every leaf a tale to tell,
Secrets held in twilight's swell.

Dimming light with every sigh,
Painting shadows in the sky.
Promises of night to come,
Beating hearts, a gentle drum.

In the dusky, fading light,
Hope ignites the coming night.
As the stars begin to gleam,
We embrace the night's soft dream.

Serenities of the Afterglow

Lingering in the afterglow,
Soft reflections start to flow.
Crimson skies and deep, calm seas,
Whisper secrets on the breeze.

Moments pause, then drift away,
Caught in twilight's gentle sway.
Each heartbeat echoes through the mist,
In this peace, we dare to exist.

Nature sings a lullaby,
As stars begin to dot the sky.
Every sigh a wish we keep,
In the stillness, hearts will leap.

Let the afterglow embrace,
With each fading light, a trace.
Finding solace in the night,
Guiding dreams to take their flight.

Transition into Tranquility

Drifting clouds in pale blue skies,
Soothe the world with gentle sighs.
Time stands still, the heartbeats blend,
In the hush where shadows mend.

Golden rays begin to fade,
Drawing lines where dreams are laid.
Whispers weave a soft embrace,
Filling hearts with boundless grace.

Every moment flows like streams,
Carrying hopes and quiet dreams.
In this space, we find our own,
A sanctuary gently grown.

Transition to a calm delight,
As day slips into velvet night.
In the quiet, we unite,
Finding peace in shared twilight.

Milton Keynes UK
Ingram Content Group UK Ltd.
UKHW021629011224
451755UK00010B/524